T0149727

KEEP YOUR CHIN UP

LINDA LENDT

BALBOA.
PRESS

A DIVISION OF HAY HOUSE

Balboa Press books may be ordered through booksellers or by contacting:

Balboa Press
A Division of Hay House
1663 Liberty Drive
Bloomington, IN 47403
www.balboapress.com
1 (877) 407-4847

Print information available on the last page.

ISBN: 978-1-5043-4510-1 (sc)
ISBN: 978-1-5043-4511-8 (e)

Library of Congress Control Number: 2015919102

Balboa Press rev. date: 12/17/2015

Contents

Part III: Health

Part IV: Revelations

Part V: Worth Sharing

Introduction

Keep Your Chin Up is about my life, lessons I've learned and things worth sharing that helped me see value in everything and put my life into perspective. Positive thinking and gratitude were my aids along the way.

I hope this book will help you evaluate your life and look for the messages from the universe each day. It will open your mind to your very own God-self, which is waiting to be discovered, appreciated and nurtured.

Linda Lendt

To my family and friends, with a special thanks to my daughter Candy for all her technical support and computer skills. Also, I'd like to extend additional gratitude to Renee and Karen for their consistent moral support and feedback.

Foreword

This little book is, for the most part, true. It was a labour of love that I wanted to share with my family and friends. Some of my stories are embellished a bit to enhance readability and humour. The thoughts conveyed are a keepsake of a lifestyle you may never understand, but I hope you get to know another side of me and learn from the experiences of my youth.

My character has been exposed in the printing of this book. My aim was to put things in writing before cobwebs clouded my mind—just enjoy it!

PART I

Observations

1. My Humble Beginning and My Life as a Parent

This is the story of me. I was born in Haileybury, Ontario. On a stormy, miserable day, I decided to show myself to the world.

The day was May 30, 1952, and it was 2:00 a.m. My dad had just gone to harness the horses to take my mother to the hospital. I can't even imagine having to ride in a buckboard while starting labour. At that time, my dad did not have a vehicle, and we lived half a mile off the main road. (This almost sounds like *Little House on the Prairie* as I recount the story!)

When my dad came back in from the barn, it was too late: I was on my way, and he had to deliver me. He said that he had never been so scared in all his life. The fact that he had to deliver his own baby was unnerving; luckily, however, he had farm experience. And obviously, he did a fine job ... because I am here today!

Anyway, I flourished as the youngest of seven children in our country family. Aunt Kathryn named me because she didn't have any children of her own and always wanted a daughter. She called me Linda Marie. I like the name— except for the fact that it was so common back then.

I am a left-handed person, which can be a little difficult at times in a right-handed world. My writing has always been composed at an awful angle or started at the edge of the page and ended up on the far side when writing a column. I started on the left side of addition columns instead of the right side, and the sums never added up. The advantage to being a left-handed person, though, is that it triggers the creative side of my brain, which has bestowed a great imagination upon me. I enjoy my creativity because I have always had a knack for seeing things from a fresh perspective. I see animation in almost all inanimate objects. It also brings out my joie de vivre. I've heard experts say, "Left-handed people are the only ones in their right minds." Sometimes, when I feel awkward, I think of that quotation and smile.

As of the time of this writing, I am a mother and a grandmother. My children are all grown, and the blessings of being a grandparent are mine to enjoy. Parenting is the hardest job a person will ever have, but it is also the most rewarding. It is a job that lasts as long as you live and as long as you have a heart with which you can care and love.

Newborn babies are such mysterious miracles. It does not matter how many new ones I see—I marvel at each new life. Babies are usually quite easy to care for during the earliest stage, unless they have health problems. Such was the case with my granddaughter Amy. Shortly after she was born, she turned blue frequently. The doctors could not find the cause, but they thought formula might be getting into her lungs. That mystery was never solved, but after three months, the problem went away. I was not willing to watch Amy during that time. I was afraid she would do her little Smurf trick, as I called it, and turn blue. I took care of her plenty after that, though, without incident.

As children become toddlers, they are more fun to care for. I love getting little ones to say big words. Just watching their facial expressions is a hoot. This is the age when their personalities develop, and if you are a part of their lives, it is an extraordinary privilege. Stimulating the minds of children can be a delightful surprise when they exhibit extraordinary talent with a fresh outlook on the matter. I believe that children between the ages of one and ten are the most impressionable, and I have always sought to help them grow during those formative years. They like to help, and adults should not discourage their efforts.

Teenagers can be complex, hormonal beings, but I enjoy them as well. They need their space, but they also need a willing ear to listen to their problems. I was always there for my children—and their friends as well. My daughter's friends thought I was "so cool," which is a compliment that I still value highly. Patience, discipline and respect are the main necessities for healthy teenagers.

When my daughter Calico was in grade 12, we held the graduation party at our home in the country. Everyone was telling me I was crazy, that the kids would wreck everything. I did not believe they would. What surprised me was that no other parent in the area was willing to hold this honorary event for the grads. We were new to the area, but there would not have been a graduation party that year if my husband and I had not consented.

We only had two days to organize the event. My youngest daughter, Hollie, who was 14 at the time, talked to her friends about a band, and the event was advertised by word of mouth. The night of the party, at least one thousand kids showed up. We lost track after that, but there was not an empty patch of grass to be seen. I am very proud to say that there were no casualties, save one lawn chair that became a burnt offering on the bonfire. Again, I believe that because I respected the kids, they showed respect in return. I would host the party again in a minute.

In closing, I would like to say that people are people; it does not matter whether they are large or small, young or old. Indeed, everyone has feelings that need to be considered. Children need guidance and rules, but we must not forget to respect them. And in return, we will be loved and respected.

2. My dog – Lady

Lady, come here. Lady where are you? She is my dog, my special friend. We live in the country and there is not many kids to play with the around here. I spend a lot of time with Lady. I have taught her to sing, dance, rollover, whisper, shake a paw, and sit up. The neatest thing of all- she talks on the phone to me when I am away from home. Sometimes I call just to talk to her. It sounds like AWOO-WOO,WOO! It just makes me happy.

"Richard have you seen Lady this morning? I want to say goodbye to her before I leave for school."

"No I haven't seen her since last night. She was laying in the yard by the barn chewing on a big bone, Linda, the bus will be here in about five minutes".

"Tell them I'm sick! I'm not going! I can't leave without seeing her." This is not like Lady, she always comes when I call.

I was the only one home now, and my mind was racing, thinking the worst. What if she is hurt, lost or stolen. She usually stayed on our property. I would see her out in the field catching frogs. It was quite entertaining to see. Her body looked like it was on puppet strings, as she pounced up and down trying to catch a frog.

Somebody had dropped Lady off as a stray, 2 years earlier. It was hard to find a home for female puppies, so my dad let me keep, now she's my best friend.

I saddled my horse, then I started on my quest. There is a 20 acre field behind our barn. I skirted all around it, calling her name. Nothing!

I started to cry. I am only 15 and I can't imagine life without her. I headed up the road to my neighbors, to see if they had and unknown visitor.

"Hello Mr. Lafleur, Have you seen a stray dog here today?"

"What does it look like?"

"She Is the color of coffee with lots of cream in and she looks like she's smiling. Her eyes are bright and brown."

"No sorry, There were a couple bothering my sheep, they were black with brown spots. I fired my gun in their direction and they left pretty quick. I don't think they'll be back. I may just have hit one."

"O, k. thanks".

It was a good thing that I was on my horse Jody. My legs felt like rubber, I thought I was going to faint. I talked to Jody all the way home trying to console myself. The day was half over and I still did not find her. I knew I had to ride the cow trails through the bush next. But, I was scared.

There were a lot of black bears, back there and if they have babies, they are very protective of them. I will just leave a note on the table saying where I am, just in case something happens. I am asking God to help me be brave. I just love my dogs so much I would do anything to find her.

I strained my eyes and ears for some clue of my dog's whereabouts. Overshadowed by trees and forests sounds like squirrels chattering in the trees and the snap of falling branches, I tensed up. Nature is beautiful but it can be so unpredictable.

I called Lady again. I came to the end of the trail, and a bird flew out of the bushes, startling my horse. He bolted sideways and bucked, knocking me to the ground. I landed in between two trees. I felt lightheaded and a little shaky. It was a good thing that Jody's ground trained. That means that when you drop the reins, the horse will not run away because it thinks that it is tied.

I was right near the beaver pond, and I said out loud to myself-"How I'm going to find her now Jody"

I got up slowly, and walked towards the pond. I wanted to wait a few minutes before riding again. I bent over to pick up of Marsh Merrigolds. They are my favorite, color, bright yellow and I was trying to cheer myself up. Out of the corner of my eye, I saw something cream-colored at the edge of the water. It was extremely swampy in that area, so I had to be careful that I didn't get bogged down. I found a knarled stick, and used it like it a cane to check the sturdiness of the ground. I stepped gingerly and parted the reeds by the water. I gasped, my dog was laying there motionless, with her foot caught in a muskrat trap. I patted her, and soothed her. She looked up at me with dull eyes, she didn't even lift head or wag her tail. It was like she was giving up. I had to go get help. Her back left leg was caught just above t he paw. There was no way that I could squeeze a trap open to free her by myself.

With a sense of urgency, I mounted my horse and rode as fast as I could, keeping my body low so I didn't get a branch in the eye. As I came into the clearing, I saw the school bus passing by my house, so I knew that my brother was home.

"Richard, I need your help! Lady is caught in a trap!"

"Oh no! I will meet you at the barn"

"I will saddle Pierre."

"I'll get a blanket to wrap Lady in."

I tried to stay calm as we freed her from the trap. Richard squeezed it open, tissues of the leg were mangled and bloody, showing signs of a struggle, but the bone was not broken. A muskrat, will chew their own leg just to be free of a trap.

Richard wrapped Lady in a blanket and carefully lifted her up to me. So I could drape her across my lap. She lay there like a limp rag.

My heart was aching, but I calmed myself. God helped me find her. We traveled slowly and by time we got back, my dad was home from work. He loaded her into the seat of the truck and we headed straight to the vet clinic.

"She is lucky, "the vet said. She is weak, and she has lost a lot of blood. She will be sore for a while, I'm giving you a bottle of "Detol" to soak that leg. It must be done every day, twice a day for two weeks. Throw in some TLC and I predict that lady will be her old self in no time."

3. Who Took My Pants?

January 11, 1997, started out as a glorious day. It was the day that Cynthia, my niece, was joined in holy wedlock to the love of her life, Darren. I had travelled from London to attend this family occasion as a guest, but I was also the makeup artist, which went well.

The sun shone brightly, lighting up the sparkling snow, warming the winter air and touching this special day with promise. The guests arrived, and the ceremony began. The flower girl, dressed like a delicate china doll in her white dress, came down the aisle gingerly. Looking up, her shyness overcame her, and she stopped. One of the bridesmaids walked up beside her and tucked the girl's trembling hand in hers, and together they continued down the aisle. That went well.

The bride, a vision of elegance who looked like she had just stepped off a page of *Vogue* magazine, beamed with happiness as she proceeded down the aisle. Satin, lace, pearls and Cinderella-style pumps accentuated her beauty. Her nerves were steady, and she and her fiancé said their vows. That went well.

The wedding party looked its best: beautiful dresses; impressive tailored tuxedos; trailing bouquets of purple, white, and lavender flowers; and loving smiles on all the faces.

Up to that point, the day was without flaw. Dining, dancing and conversing made the time fly. History was made, and then it was time to go home. Tired and wishing to relax, the bride and groom returned to their suite to enjoy the benefits of their union. Turning the key in the lock, the door creaked and yielded slowly. What a state of dishevelment came into view!

Layers of rice were lumped between the sheets, the available clothes were tied in knots, toilet paper was wrapped around every drawer and Vaseline covered the washroom facilities. And the story gets better. The Jacuzzi tub was filled with fresh ice cubes, and the inviting bottle of wine had been dumped and refilled with water.

Cynthia had had enough. She just wanted to slip out of her Cinderella dress and into the comfortable, forgiving, loose pair of track pants she had brought with her. "Where are they?" she asked. "Where did they go? Somebody must have taken them! But who?"

By then, we were all back at our designated lodgings, enjoying the company of our families and winding down. And that's when the phone rang. It was Cynthia, wanting to know whether her track pants had ended up in my belongings when I had packed up to leave the room after doing her and her bridesmaids' makeup.

"No," I said, "I'm positive I don't have them."

"Okay, thanks," she said with confusion in her voice.

My sister, Irene, said, "Linda, maybe you should check, just in case."

"No," I said, "there is no reason to check. I know that I didn't take them."

"Come on," Irene pleaded, "what will it hurt to look?"

"Okay," I agreed, "I will check if it makes you happy."

I got my bag and pulled out the contents, unconcerned: two shirts, a black slip, plaid pyjamas, two pairs of jeans and …

My chin dropped as my heart palpitated and my eyes widened. I stammered, trying to find the appropriate words, and I dreaded making the phone call. I looked guilty, but my conscience was clear. Meanwhile, back at the hotel, Cynthia was wrapped in a bedsheet, lacking any suitable attire for relaxation.

I contemplated jumping in my car and heading for home, humbled by embarrassment and surprised that I too had been set up. But I didn't.

Ultimately, Cynthia forgave me and still calls me her aunt—thankfully!

4. Monday

Do you ever wonder why, on some days, things just don't go smoothly? This is a story of such a day.

The day started in an ordinary, calm way. It was Monday morning. I got up, drank a cup of coffee, and while I ate my breakfast, I made a mental note regarding what I needed to do. I was heading to town to run some errands and buy a pair of shoes.

I was going to repair a horse blanket for my niece, but it required laundering first. I went to pick up the blanket from the deck and put it in my car. I peeked at the contents in the bag to be sure that I had the right one. *That's it,* I said to myself, *I can see the red at the top.*

I jumped in my car and started off with a great sense of efficiency. This feeling did not last long. My first stop was at my neighbour's house to drop off some money for Avon products that I had ordered. While I was planning my second stop, I realized that I had forgotten to stop to pay my neighbour. Five minutes later, I remembered. *No biggie,* I thought, *I'll do it on the way home.*

I figured that I should go to the laundromat first and wash the blanket. *This way,* I mused, *I can leverage my time by going to pick out my shoes while the blanket is being washed.* Once I found the right change for the washer and inserted the coins, I opened the bag to dump the blanket in. Instead of the blanket, however, out fell various pieces of clothing, including a red sweater. *Oh no!* I thought, *Wrong bag! But it's no biggie; I'll just give the complimentary cycle in the readied machine to a stranger and leave.*

I continued on to purchase my shoes. I drove around trying to find a parking spot until spying one that required me to parallel park, which I don't usually do. I had just stepped inside the shoe store with a big grin on my face, when it dawned on me that I had left my money at home. Every intention of efficiency had been replaced with constant blunders.

My next errand was to drop off some jars at an address on May Street. "You can't miss it," my sister, Rita, said. "The number might be hard to see, but there is a black utility trailer in the yard." Needless to say, it was not where I thought it was. I inquired around the neighbourhood, but no one was sure of the correct location of the house I was searching for. This was typical of my day so far, so I didn't panic. I had four boxes of jars rattling in protest in the back seat of my car, so I went to a public phone booth and looked up the proper street number. At that moment, I breathed a sigh of relief and thought, *At least this time it was not my mistake!* I happily delivered the jars.

There was one errand that did go well that morning. I had to return a book to the library. It was too big to fit in the return slot, but the library was open.

Returning home, the rest of the day passed without any additional problems. Reflecting on these incidents, I became more appreciative of how little things can make a big difference.

PART II

The Lighter Side

5. Pink Popcorn

Back in the fifties, when I was a young girl, we lived in the country. My dad drove a pickup truck, and seating in the vehicle was limited. There were seven children in our family, so it was impossible to fit all of us in the cab of the truck at the same time. In the nice weather, four of us could hop in the back for the great pleasure of going to town. My dad would let us stay in the parking lot, providing we conducted ourselves properly and stayed in the back of the truck. We all happily agreed as he went off to buy groceries, promising a treat for all of us on his return. It was one of our great childhood delights. Because we never knew when Daddy would come around the corner, we didn't misbehave and risk him catching us in a moment of questionable behaviour, which would cause him to revoke our treat privileges. We never knew for sure what our reward would be. It could be chips, chocolate bars, or our favorite: pink popcorn. Whenever we saw my dad coming to the truck with popcorn in his hands, we all sang, "Here comes Daddy with the pink popcorn! Here comes Daddy with the pink popcorn! Here comes Daddy with the *pink popcorn!*"

These antics seem rather silly now, but the thought of that popcorn still brings a smile to my face, and the happy memory warms my heart. This anecdote reminds me of the joys and simplicities of childhood.

6. There's a Bear

Growing up in northern Ontario, there was no shortage of wildlife encounters. One dark, stormy evening during my teen years, I woke up to the roar of gusting winds and clapping thunder. I jumped out of my bed and went to the window to close it. Peering out, I saw a bear at our outhouse door. It seemed to me that he was trying to tear the door off of its hinges. My brother and I were the only ones home at the time, so I bolted into his room and blurted, "Richard, there is a bear at the toilet door!"

Sleepily, he gazed out the window, and then, without a word, he got dressed, grabbed his gun and headed out the door. In fearful anticipation, I watched while I muttered out loud, "Please, Lord, don't let that bear hurt my brother." My eyes followed every step he took.

Suddenly, halfway there, he turned around and came back in the house while laughing. "Why are you coming back in? What is so funny? He is still there."

"Linda," he replied, "look again." So I did. I began to chuckle too. The trees beside the outhouse were whipping in the wind, bending back and forth with such intensity and at regular intervals that they resembled the body of a black bear. Through the power of suggestion, my brother saw the same apparition that I did. We still laugh about the incident today and marvel at the strange powers of the mind.

7. Looks Can Be Deceiving

It was my daughter Calico's 15th birthday, so I made her favorite cake: Black Forest. We lit the candles and sang "Happy Birthday." I dished out the treat of the day, but as soon as the kids took a bite, they all cried, "Blah! Yuck!" I could not believe that something that looked so good could taste so awful. I had forgotten to add the sugar to my recipe. After I realized my blunder, my husband told the kids that there was money in the cake. They all dug into the cake with their hands to find the cash, but there wasn't any.

I wanted to get rid of the evidence of my mistake, so I gave it to the dog, but not even *he* would even eat it. Many years and many cakes later, that birthday cake is still my most memorable one.

8. Chewing Inhibited

I wear dentures. Firm, juicy apples are out of the question in their natural state. To take a bite of one would result in my top denture breaking off, and it would be looking back at me atop the apple that I was trying to eat. Instead, I must control my urge and reach for a knife to cut off a portion of it. Peanuts, which I love, cause discomfort because they get under the bridgework, prodding and digging into my gums.

When I want to eat a salad, I must first consider what kind it is, and then I must contemplate how much time I have. You see, these store-bought choppers are dull as can be. They are more for cosmetic purposes than anything else. When I feel a sneeze coming on, my instinct is to cover my mouth—not only because it is good manners, but also because my teeth might go flying out like a ball of metal propelled from a cannon. My biggest annoyance occurs when I want to yell: I can form only certain syllables with my lips or my dentures will be jump out of my mouth.

Ill-fitting dentures can irritate the gums and cause painful canker sores, which make it difficult to eat or speak properly. In short, even though I can make light of this disability, it is one with which I must contend.

9. Keep Still

My grandfather gained a reputation for being a great fisherman and woodsman. He was very skilled in the outdoors, and his gardening skills were excellent. I was 7 years old when he passed away. I still remember him going to town in the winter with his old horse hitched to the double-runner sleigh. He always stopped on his way home to give his grandkids pink peppermints or ice cream.

He was a man who taught me respect for my elders. As a young child, I was always babbling about anything I could think of. During those times, he would tell me to keep still. I would sit as still as possible, but I kept yakking. I did not know that *keep still* meant that I should be quiet. From that time on, I honoured his wishes because, often, my chatter was bothersome to older people.

10. Moose Lake

I close my eyes and see it still: the home of my grandfather, the place of my birth, the most special part of my world.

Moose Lake is shielded from view, set back a half a mile from the main road. If you are lucky enough to look at just the right moment while travelling along the main road, you will catch a glimpse of the enticing blue water through the protective pines.

I remember my grandfather's luscious, coveted carrot patch vividly. As youngsters, my siblings and I always tried to pilfer a few of those tasty treasures. Somehow, as if he had superhuman hearing, my grandpa would always catch us and wag a stick at us disapprovingly. He also had rhubarb that grew abundantly. We were allowed to help ourselves to it. Breaking off the leaves, we would then peel the red skin back and plaster the stock with salt. We crunched happily while our mouths tingled at the tartness of the fruit.

When we had finished our chores, we tramped along the hardened trails close to the lake. We trekked through the sharp, prickly brush to find bushes laden with bright red pin cherries. They are tiny and very tart. Chokecherries hung heavily on bushes. When they were ripe, they were a dull black and the size of blueberries. We had to be careful not to eat too many, though, because we didn't want our teeth to turn brown.

Because the lake was so calm, we were allowed to take the canoe out (unsupervised) to fish for yellow perch or to check the muskrat traps. We would sit there and listen to the caw of a crow flying by or the slap of a fish jumping out of the water. We could feel the canoe wiggle when a breeze caressed the side of it. Jack pine trees stood on guard along the shores; they were tall, intimidating and thickly clustered. Pinecones were hanging like corsages, and they were held together with nature's glue: pine gum. The pine scent from the trees, mixed with the musty earth aroma and the fishy water imprinted a lasting impression of good country air and healthy living on me.

In all its untamed, natural abundance, Moose Lake is still a tranquil, picturesque place in my mind. It will always be special in my heart; after all, it is also the place where I was born.

11. 1 + 1 = 4

When I was 8 years old, I liked school. Still, I had an extremely low tolerance for and understanding of arithmetic. This is a story of the valuable lesson I learned when I tried to balk at the system.

At the end of the day, we were assigned two pages of grade-3 arithmetic homework. It was to be completed by the following morning. The problem was that I could not justify missing an entertaining show on TV or playing outside. Plain and simple, I did not want to do my homework; therefore, I devised what I thought was a foolproof plan to avert this despicable task.

On my bus ride home, I plotted my course of action. I rushed into my bedroom and threw my books on the bed. Quickly, I found my textbook, located the assigned pages and removed the evidence from the text. I was trying to be quiet so my sisters would not notice me misbehaving. The *crack-crack* sound of the printed evidence pulling away seemed amplified, but the caper was a success. I stashed the pages under a cushion, as if they were stolen loot. And then I went out to play.

The next day, I went to school and soberly professed to my teacher that I could not do my homework because I did not have the correct pages in my book. The reaction I got was totally unexpected. Mrs. Plaunt's face became violently red, her cheeks puffed up and the words spurted from her lips like a balloon hissing out air: "Young lady," she bellowed, "they most certainly were. I checked all of the books myself at the beginning of the year. Just let me discuss this with your older sister." She then marched hastily out of the classroom to find my sister.

That night, Irene interrogated me until I confessed. My eyes spouted with tears of regret and I blurted in a shaky voice, "I hid them under the couch cushion." There wasn't much said after that. Irene picked up the crinkled pieces of paper and put them in her school bag.

Upon receiving the evidence of my fumbled effort, Mrs. Plaunt taught me a lesson I will never forget. She assigned me four pages of arithmetic homework to be completed by the next day instead of the original two. On that day, I made a silent oath to do my homework as originally assigned, *no matter what.*

12. Spending Time with My Dad

When I was younger, my dad sold firewood to make extra income. On weekends, he went into the bush to cut trees and haul them out so they could cure and be sold as firewood.

On one miserable Saturday, I asked to accompany him. He said that the weather was not too warm for a young girl like me, but I begged to go, so he relented. He warned me, though: "Don't be whining and complaining that you are cold. We are going to be gone all day."

"I won't," I replied eagerly.

We set out, bundled in wool coats, warm scarves and felt-lined boots. I was also armed with a great deal of optimism. The wind lashed mercilessly while I sat on the sleigh, trying to enjoy the beauty of nature around me. The team of horses plodded on, leaving behind the deep, indentations of the runner tracks of the sleigh. After about half an hour into the journey, my dad turned and asked, "How you doing back there, kid?" I didn't want to tell him that I was freezing, so I stated, "I'm okay. How much longer until we are there?" My dad replied, "If you are cold, you can walk behind the sleigh to warm up."

"Good idea," I answered as I jumped down and followed until we reached our destination. The forest surrounded us, except for the clearing where a neat pile of logs was placed. Even though we were shielded from the weather somewhat, it was still extremely cold. As the day wore on, we stopped to have some lunch, which consisted of roast beef sandwiches and oatmeal cookies. To complement our snack, we drank some bush tea—nothing fancy, just black, loose-leaf tea chucked into a tin pail of boiling water. Being there by the heat of the fire and sipping tea warmed my insides. I felt happy to be there; it made me forget about the cold that gripped me.

By that evening, my face was flushed by the masterful wind and my appendages numb, but as my body thawed and tingled, I looked upon it as a good day that I got to spend with my dad.

13. Stump and Peanut

As a child, I was always big for my age. I was even bigger than my brother, Richard, who was a year older than I was. This is how the nicknames *Stump* and *Peanut* originated. Old Tommy, as we called him, nicknamed me Stump. He said that I was so big that I must have crawled out from under a stump. My brother was scrawny and short, so Old Tommy dubbed him Peanut. He was so small, the argument went, that he must have come from a peanut shell. It was a great joke to the insensitive men who worked for my dad, but I did not share their opinion.

To this day, if a nickname is not funny or complimentary, I will not use it. It is so true what they say about words being more powerful than swords: physical wounds will heal, but emotional scars can last a lifetime.

14. *Gofor* Wood

As a young girl, I always looked up to my older brother. Everything that he told me, I accepted as truth. One day, I really saw the light! While working on a grade-7 project about different types of trees, I had to gather pieces of bark to identify each species. Striving for excellence, I asked my brother, Rene, for help identifying one particular tree. He told me it was *gofor* wood. I diligently wrote down the following words: birch, maple, cedar, tamarac, balsam and *gofor* wood onto a sheet of bristle board. I then glued the appropriate sample beside it.

Upon completion, I turned in my project and waited excitedly for the results. After all, my big brother, in all his wisdom, had assisted me. Luckily, the assignment was only worth ten marks. Expecting a perfect score, I was very dissatisfied with a score of six out of ten. Plus, there was a large, red question mark beside the words *gofor wood.*

Pursing my lips and holding back my disappointment, I went directly to my sibling and confronted him. "Rene, you told me that this type of wood is *gofor* wood! The teacher marked it wrong." I said sadly. "He told me that it is called poplar,"

With a mischievous grin, Rene replied, "It is *gofor* wood. You throw a stick on the fire and go like hell for more."

15. Lucky Turn

I will always remember a particular fall day a few years ago, when fog as thick as a big bag of polyester stuffing made driving safety questionable. Dreariness enveloped our vision as I pulled out of the driveway to take my husband, Gary, back to work.

I figured that, if I went slowly, I would be safe. It was only a half-mile drive. I was making a left turn. We strained our eyes but could not see or hear any oncoming traffic. I prayed as I pulled the truck onto the road. Not even ten seconds went by before a truck was coming from the opposite direction. The truck was navigating without headlights in a horrible fog. The pickup was so close I could have touched it without extending my arm much. My heart was gripped with churning fear. *What if I had waited just a few more seconds before pulling out? Would I be here to tell the tale?*

16. House Fire

February 21, 1996, is a day I will never forget. It has been burned into my mind. On that day, our home burnt to the ground. Only by the grace of God, am I able to sit here and relay the story to you.

At 2:00 a.m. on that morning, I stirred as an undeniable force was shaking me awake. I could hear "Wake up! Wake up!" but my mind was saying, "No, I don't want to wake up. I'm so tired." I had gotten home late the night before and was exhausted. I was trying to ignore the pain in my back, so I swallowed two tablets of Tylenol and two muscle relaxants before dropping into bed for a night of painless slumber. By then, it was 12:30 a.m.

The force would not go away. I could feel a huge hand shaking my shoulder with dogged determination. Finally, I stirred to a conscious level and my nose detected an unexplainable stench. I mumbled to myself, "Okay, I'll get up. I can smell something. Maybe one of my girls left the iron on and it overheated." I was not too concerned because the laundry room was next to our bedroom. With my eyes partially open, I scuttled into the room to solve the problem. Everything was copacetic there. My mind was willing, but my body was not. I wanted nothing more than to go back to sleep. My foggy brain started to clear, however, because the annoying, sleep-depriving odour was not going away.

I proceeded into the living room and was shocked awake as if ten gallons of cold water had been thrown on me. The entire kitchen in front of me was raging bonfire. My instincts kicked in, and I knew what I needed to do. My two teenage daughters and a friend of the family were asleep on the next floor, so I ran halfway up the stairs and yelled, "Get up! The house is on fire!" I screamed, detected movement and knew that my children were aware of a terrifying crisis by the pitch of my voice. I then charged down the stairs to make sure that our escape would be possible and unobstructed. Dave, StarrAnne and Hollie stumbled as they came down the stairs and made it out.

As a lover of pets, StarrAnne tried to get our dog, Duke, out, but the terrified animal bolted away from her. My husband, Gary, was able to grab Duke, but he wriggled away from him too. We fled from the haze and the engulfing flames, out the back door to safety.

It was like two different worlds: the fiery furnace of hell and the freezing cold of the North Pole. Standing there, with just pyjamas on, barefoot in the snow, we were too shocked to shiver.

Even though I realized everyone was accounted for, I bellowed, "Where are you, Hollie?" Standing not ten feet away from me, she blurted, "I am right here, Mom." In one last attempt to save Duke, StarrAnne headed toward the door. I composed myself and grabbed the back of her nightgown to stop her. The knob was untouchable, and the house was inaccessible. The neighbours had called the fire department, and they were already there when we made our way outside. Planted in the snow like statues, we stared at the firemen trying to tame the consuming flames.

"You're lucky," one of them said. "Five more minutes and all of you would have died from smoke inhalation."

For two years after the fire, I was not able to drive by an innocent campfire without the smell of the smoke triggering a sickening feeling in the pit of my stomach.

I firmly believe that it was my guardian angel that warned me of the danger and saved my family from tragedy. I count my blessings every day.

17. Lessons Learned

I ask myself, *why am I writing this section of this book? Why do I feel so compelled to do this?* The reason is that I want to help others. I found a purpose and devised a plan.

I am an eternal optimist, and I can usually see the positive side of adversity, but I must admit that there are times when I feel the pull of despair. I use my creativity and overactive imagination to brighten my world. I think of my dear friend Karen as my mentor. I have seen her use the power of the universe to manifest her goals and dreams. I also picked a hero, Wonder Woman, played by Lynda Carter, to mold my new vigorous self. I picked her because we have the same first name and some of the same physical attributes: dark hair, pretty faces and voluptuous figures. She was a symbol of Amazon supremacy in a world of ordinary mortals. This TV series aired from 1975 to 1979.

When you are manifesting results in your life, you need to be specific. I had followed all the rules, picking the day, the month and the year that I wanted things to happen. I wrote it all down to solidify it in my mind, and to show the universe that I was serious about getting what I wanted.

I study all the great authors that I can, such as Wayne Dyer, James Arthur Ray and Jack Canfield, to name a few. These men are all enlightened and offer instructions and affirmations that anyone can learn if they hunger for a more fulfilling life.

I have always said that nothing could take away my joie de vivre, but I almost had to eat my words at one point. I changed my thoughts and reprogrammed my thinking to see the spiritual design of it all.

Life without humour is boring, and I hope that, by offering the lighter side of adversity, you may realize that, even when tragedy becomes reality, life is still worthwhile. Breathe in, breathe out, life is good. It is my wish that you will find threads of hope and direction in these pages that will lead you in new directions and that you will glean new insights about your life.

PART III

Health

18. Tragedy Strikes

On May 19, 2007, I woke up with a sense of familial love and pride. I was thinking about how quickly time had passed, and the fact that, now that my children are grown, I have the privilege of being a grandmother and great-grandmother.

We were celebrating Mother's Day, my birthday and my two grandsons' birthdays. We lump the events together to accommodate everyone's schedules. Today was the day we were supposed to honour our mothers. The truth is that I want to honour mine, but she didn't give me much to work with. I realize that, when I think about her, the inside of my heart is heavy with regret. She left when I was 2 years old, and I do not know much about her thoughts or character. I guess that is why I feel so strongly about being here for my kids, even though they are grown. After all, you never outgrow the need for approval or advice from your parents. I didn't, at least. Until the end, my dad was the world to me.

We arrived at Calico's home at 4:30 p.m. I was happy. I walked up onto the porch and started the party off with a bang! The toe of my sandal got caught in a small tear in the carpet, which caused me to fall forward and strike my head on the brick wall on the way down. I had fallen many times in my life, but I could always get back up on my own in the past. This time, though, I could not move! My arms and legs felt like they belonged to someone else. I could not will them to move. Also, I had the misguided perception that my appendages were suspended in the air. I lay there alone for about one minute until my daughter Hollie came around the corner with the rest of the stuff from the car. She squealed and shrieked like a scared rabbit, which got the attention of everyone inside.

The easiest and most important step, calling 911, was carried out, but the shock of that fall reverberated quite a bit. Curiously, I was very calm, but I kept repeating to myself, *Help me, God! Help me, Bruno!* (When I refer to Bruno, I mean Bruno Groening. He lived in Germany and was known as a spiritual healer who lived from 1906 to 1959.) This helped me. I was surprised that I could not get up, but not once did I blame God for what had happened to me.

I laid on the porch for 45 minutes before the paramedics were able to get me on the stretcher. They said I kept crying out in pain every time they tried to move me. The mind is kind—I don't recall an unbearable amount of discomfort. Finally, I said to the attendants, "Don't worry about me, just do what you were trained to do in a situation like this." In approximately five minutes, they had me on the stretcher, headed for the local hospital.

The doctors there determined that I needed emergency surgery. The staff made many calls to find a suitable hospital that had a surgery opening. Finally, they decided that I would go to the Hamilton General Hospital.

I don't remember a lot about the following two weeks. I just know that the doctor explained to me that I had an incomplete spinal cord injury. It was not completely severed, so it might repair itself. That was great news! For the first time in my life, incomplete was not a reference to my homework!

The surgeon fused my C 3-4 and C 5-6 vertebrae, which are located high in the neck. The prognosis was that I might walk again, but it would take at least two years for my body to recover.

19. The Reality of It All

It took a ten-second fall to take it all away: my movement, my freedom and my fun with my children and grandchildren. I lost my ability to drive, my ability to wash and dress myself, my ability to do crafts on my own and my ability to sew and cook for myself. I even lost the freedom to choose what time to get up, go to bed, or take a shower.

Before the fall, I prided myself on my independence; now, there is not a day that I can be left alone to fend for myself. I feel like an inconvenience to my family and friends. Whenever there is a family function, it has to be coordinated around my needs, which I feel uncomfortable about.

Shopping is also limited. Even stores that are wheelchair accessible are not able to present all their shelves at a level where I can see and reach for the items I want. Also, I fear that I am losing the affection of my grandchildren—not because they don't love me, but because it scares them to see me in this wheelchair. My nature walks are also a thing of the past. I am mad, I am sad and I am angry as hell that this happened to me. I am bruised on the inside, but I smile on the outside so that the good that I have around me does not go away.

I pray every day for healing. As I write these words, it has been a 17-month ordeal. I am starting to walk with a high walker. It is a device that is as high as my armpits, and it has wheels. I hang onto grab bars at the front of it and move myself forward by moving my legs. It helps to strengthen my upper and lower body.

This is where I put things into perspective and look for the silver lining, where I try to find purpose and direction. Many years ago, I heard Lorne Green narrate a poem, "Desiderata," on the radio. It resonated with me. I feel that it was written for me because it delivers the same philosophy I believe: treat everyone with kindness and respect, and most of the time you will receive the same in return.

20. Memories

The first six months of recovery were a blur of therapy, sleeping, phlegm and Kleenex. It is said that, when you have a spinal cord injury, you sleep a lot. Plus, therapy made me tired, so I was nodding off all the time. In the big picture, that was good because it correlated with bodily repair.

For two to three months, I had to use a yankauer. This is a device used to clear the lungs of phlegm. The Kleenex was used for any leftover, unwanted moisture in and around my mouth, and the tissues became a trailing pile of white waste reaching from my hips all the way up to my armpits. One nurse commented that, when she thought of me, she immediately thought of Kleenex. That was okay with me because Kleenex is soft and useful!

21. A Kleenex Anecdote

(This story was told to me by a nurse and passed down a couple of generations.)

There was an 85-year-old woman standing up at the front of the church, speaking to the congregation. She had a problem with nasal drip, so she always had some Kleenex tucked in her bosom. As she spoke, her nose began to drain inconveniently. The lady patted frantically in search of some tissue. She forgot herself and said out loud, "There was two there this morning when I left!"

The congregation howled. Some of them did not know that she was talking about Kleenex. Her face was red!

22. A Drastic Change

I have always had issues with my hair. It always looks better in my mind than in reality. When I first wake up, I look like a baby orangutan: my hair just sits on top of my head, sticking out in every direction possible. In general, it is very fine and unruly.

One day, I had the bright idea to shave my head. It made sense to me because it would be much easier to take care of and be neater.

The hairdresser would not even consider shaving it, so I had to go to the barber. My boyfriend, Kevin, chuckled the whole time that the barber worked on me. He did not think that I would go through with it. In the end, though, we matched: we were both skinheads. I didn't have any covers at first, so I had to cut up an old T-shirt to make myself a rebel hat to protect my lid from the sun.

When I first looked in the mirror, I thought I resembled my brother, Richard, who is one year older than me. I did get some strange looks, but mostly I got compliments. The nurses said that I looked like Sinead O'Connor or Demi Moore. Those compliments made me strive to sit up straighter and taller. My children frowned upon the idea at first; they thought that it was too extreme. But once they saw the end result, they realized it was a good thing. My attitude was that it couldn't look any worse and that no matter what, it would grow back.

23. Nightmares

For the first couple of months of this ordeal, there were adjustments to be made, especially where medications were concerned. The doctor was trying to adjust my pain meds, and at the same time, he was trying to keep my leg spasms under control. When you have a spinal cord injury, parts of your body vibrate at will, like a can of paint in the blending machine at a hardware store. At first, I was not able to make them stop on my own, so I needed medications. When spasm control was mixed with pain medications in certain doses, the adverse side effect was nightmares.

They were horrible! I was strapped in my wheelchair, perched at the highest point of a shoot, like a manure boom that you see on farms. If I moved, I would fall to my certain death. I tried to reason with my mind to justify that it wasn't real, but I could hear the nurses laughing, and my daughter Calico laughing too. It was like they were waiting for me to move so I would take that final plunge.

I want to live! I told myself. I tried to make my hands move, but they were strapped to my sides. This *is real! They are trying to get rid of me.* My eyes were glued shut with fear. *What can I do?*

Still trapped in the nightmare, I woke my roommate. After all, it was an emergency. "Cindy! Cindy!" I hollered. "Please help me. I am up here in the air and can't get down. Can you ring for someone to help me?"

"No!" she said. "You are not in the air; you are in your bed."

"I don't want to die!" I said.

"Linda!" Cindy said with exasperation. "Open your eyes!"

I did, and I was astounded to see that I was in my bed and the restrictions to my movements were nothing more than tight muscles. I immediately thanked God that I was safe and that the unsettling experience that I just had was caused by a potent mixture of powerful drugs and insecurities.

During my next doctor's visit, I made it clear that my plan of care must be changed immediately. I was grateful to God that I could speak up and explain how I was feeling before there was irreparable damage done to my body.

Months earlier, my nephew, Kurt, had been hospitalized unexpectedly with a brain virus. He was in a lot of pain and in a semi comatose state, unable to communicate. He was at the mercy of the doctors. He was hallucinating: he could see fish swimming and described them very convincingly. We felt so helpless watching him. I am happy to say that he recovered completely in about three months.

As a patient, you have a right to refuse medications, and I made a wise decision to stop taking those mind-altering drugs.

The next night, I was nightmare-free and able to determine that the movements of my body that I thought were voluntary movements were really muscle spasms. Consequently, I stopped participating in them, thinking that I was helping myself get ready to walk again.

I also learned how powerful the human mind is with these words by Gandhi: "A man is but a product of his thoughts. What he thinks, he becomes." The statement gave me new insight to direct my mind toward self-healing and wellness.

24. Learning Curve

I had come to terms with the losses that I incurred after my fall, but now it was time to adjust to the reality of not being able to walk or drive a car. Still, I was being offered a new avenue of freedom: a power wheelchair. But I was still convinced that my feet controlled the speed and distance that I travelled, so I had to reprogram myself to use a joystick for navigation. When my brain was alert, I did well, but when fatigue overwhelmed me, my old habits canceled the new ... my controls were in my feet again.

One particular afternoon, I was driving along as instructed, when tiredness short-circuited my new methods, causing me to regress. My friend Karen was walking beside me, and I said to her that I needed to stop because I was tired. In my mind, I had stopped because my feet were still, but I was still moving forward.

Stop! I told myself as I proceeded to run into a couch in the lounge area. Luckily, no one was hurt, but everyone was chuckling, including me. I made light of it and said, "Now for my next trick, I will stop." And then I proceeded ahead to scrape the table and chair sitting next to the couch. It wasn't funny anymore, and I was afraid that they would take the power chair away from me. At Parkwood Hospital, if you are documented three times for dangerous driving, your power chair is taken away from you and you have to go back to a manual chair. I certainly did not want that! My hands are now my feet in the world of driving, and it is up to me to keep my driving privilege.

Another funky feature on this chair is the tilt. It allows me to spend all day in my chair without undue pain or fatigue. I can reposition myself at the push of a big, red button located on the outside of the control panel, on the left side of the chair.

One night, my roommates and I were headed down to play horse races. The three of us pilled into the elevator, all in wheelchairs, on our way to have some fun. I was closest to the entrance. Suddenly, I realized that my chair was tilting up without my help. Once it got to a certain height, I was stuck up in the air, unable to get myself down because the control button was lodged against the elevator railing, holding us all hostage and helpless on our own. When the doors opened, we all hollered for help. Someone came right away and put my chair on manual so she could push me out and end the fiasco. As soon as we got in the game room, I immediately asked the volunteer to change the tilt button to the inside of the chair, so that such an event could never happen again. I found it to be unnerving. Ultimately, I was proactive so history could not repeat itself.

25. Catheters and Suppositories

How many times have you heard the expression *hindsight is 20/20*? If I knew then what I know now, I probably would've had the surgery when the surgeon recommended it, even though they only gave me a 50 percent chance of being any better than before the surgery. But those odds didn't make me want to jump under the knife. I regret that I didn't ask more questions to find out the pros and cons of my decision.

When you have a spinal cord injury, your bladder does not function on its own. It was a sobering reality for me. For the first six months, the nurses inserted intermittent catheters. I would be on my bed with my knees up in the air and apart. The catheter tube was inserted into my urethra to drain the urine. My bladder felt so overfull that it ached and throbbed, but it would not drain on its own. This was done six times per day, but there was a drawback: my legs were so spastic that it was difficult at times for the nurses to keep them open enough to be accurate. I was repeatedly told that I was difficult to catheterize and sometimes the nurses missed three or four times in a row. This resulted in multiple bladder infections. The occupational therapist designed a prostatic for use between my knees to keep them open and more manageable. It resembled a pair of elephant ears, to fit over the knees with a dowel in between them. I called the device my elephant ears on a stick.

This worked for a while, but there were still concerns and grumbles from the caregivers, so the medical staff put an end to the intermittent catheters. They inserted a Foley catheter, which is held inside the bladder by a little balloon that is filled with sterile water to keep it in place. It drains continually. During the day, I wore a leg bag, which was strapped onto the front of my leg and emptied three to four times per day. At bedtime, the leg bag was taken off and sterilized, and the big, square night bag was placed at the side of my bed. This is my reality until such time as I am able to transfer myself onto a toilet. It has been 14 months since the Foley was inserted, but I am determined to walk again and rid myself of all catheters.

Another dose of reality is bowel care. No longer do I just go when the urge hits: it is now a two-day process. The day before the bowel movement, I take two Senokot pills to move the feces down through the bowels. On that night, I take milk of magnesia for further assistance. The next morning, I get a suppository, and within one to two hours, it is all over. I get very embarrassed at times because the body has a way of surprising you when you least expect it.

I keep doing my affirmations and meditations, seeing and feeling a healthy me. Just to keep my spirits up I say, "This is not the real me; it is just my current reality." The frustration that I feel is hard to put into words. I just know that this is all happening to my physical body and not my true, spiritual self.

When my daughter Candy called my friend Karen to tell her what had happened to me, Karen said, "Do we still have Linda?" The answer was yes!

She made me feel special, and that is what I cling to. The power of unconditional love is strong, it soothes one's bruised ego and shattered dreams. Sometimes, you may have to take a detour in your life's journey, but if you look for good, you will find it.

I found this amazing quote by Jim Rohn to help keep me focussed:

"Take 100% responsibility for your life—

You must take personal responsibility. You cannot change the circumstances, the seasons, or the wind, but you can change yourself. That is something you have charge of."

PART IV

Revelations

26. Parkwood Gardens

While at Parkwood Rehabilitation Hospital in London, Ontario, I took advantage of the beautifully manicured, serene gardens dedicated to the memory of all of veterans who fought in World War I and World War II. I spent many hours there, meditating, enjoying nature and contemplating life. Any time I was feeling down or lonely, I went outside to view God's masterpiece.

I could also shift my thoughts off myself by looking around to see those with more serious afflictions than I had. It always amazes me to see people gain back their strength and ability when their outer shell looks so broken. Determination, persistence and belief will always manifest desirable results.

One day, when I was in the garden, I was admiring the shapes and textures of my favorite rocks and trees. To me, they are mysterious, rugged and intriguing. I was lying there, contemplating and enjoying life, when I received the gift of this poem from the universe:

My Inspiration

Letters fly on the breeze and fall into my ears as words.

The wind tingles my skin and propels a vortex of gratefulness and enlightenment into my gut.

The sun warms my hands with pulsating heat, healing my body with the feeling of inspired good health.

27. Problems Turn into Blessings

When I got the news in October of 2008 that I was being sent to a nursing home, I was devastated. I felt like no one cared about me, that I was a number, not a name. I carried my bitterness with me to Marian Villa. I was trying not to let it show, but the darkness was gnawing away at my spirit, trying hard to take away my joie de vivre. I heard myself say, "I hate it here. It is awful! No one cares!" The days passed by like strangers on the street, dull and mundane, coloured with indifference.

One morning, I woke with the memory of a book I had read. It said something like the following: "You don't have to be happy with a situation; just be happy in it." In other words, try to stay positive and change what you don't like. It was at this point that I gave myself a mental slap and edited my negativity. I stopped saying, "I hate this place" and replaced my words as follows: "It is less than wonderful." And then I came up with these words: "It is just a stepping stone." I didn't know what or how things were going to change, but I felt better with that choice of words. It raised my vibrations to attract better circumstances from the universe. Once I started to show love and respect for myself, God showered me with more blessings.

My father used to say, "If you want others to think well of you, you need to think well of yourself." I know this to be true.

I was worried about my body not getting enough therapy while I was in the nursing home, when an earth angel showed up in the form of a cleaning lady. She told me about an amazing physiotherapist who had helped her daughter. The problem was that I would have to pay her, but I didn't have the money for that at the time. My new friend Jovanka encouraged me to ask her anyway because she felt sure that she would help me. I was skeptical. In the meantime, my daughter Hollie called my lawyer's office to see whether there was any way I could get finances from my pending insurance claim. The answer was no, unless the physiotherapist was willing to wait for her money, when the claim was settled. *What are the chances of that? Slim!* I thought. Lo and behold, she agreed to an IOU. I felt divinely blessed to find someone in this day and age who actually cared enough about her patients to delay payment. I was elated. She is the type of therapist who works on the body from the inside out, reconnecting the brain with body movements, stimulating the muscles in the proper places to retrain the body to walk again. It is called deep-brain stimulation. She also helps me use my fine motor skills. My body is feeling relief, my functions are improving and I have hope for the future.

28. My New Friend

My prayer was answered. I needed a friend to talk to, play cards with and hang out with. The universe gifted me with a beautiful, vibrant, 85-years-young lady, named Claris. I met her in the dining room when she was seated at my table. We bonded almost immediately because we had card playing and sewing in common. We started making cushions and playing cards that first week.

We have developed a good rapport, like a mother and daughter. Claris has a daughter around my age, and she lives in Alberta, so our relationship filled a void for her as well. We play cards, almost every night. It makes being here more bearable. God gave me a lasting friendship, and I am very grateful for that.

Death and taxes are certain in this life, but so is change. I found myself longing for a better quality of life. I had heard that the government had started a pilot project for people with disabilities. They were selecting individuals who were being cared for in nursing homes, individuals who were forced to be there prematurely due to system overload and deficiencies—too young to be in such an atmosphere, yet to needy to be on their own without assistance. I was contacted by an organization called the Cheshire Assisted-LivingProgram.

This program allows individuals to live on their own with scheduled help coming in throughout the day and night to attend to their needs as required. It encourages self-sufficiency and gives the recipient a better quality of life. I was so thankful to be in this program. I had been injected with hope and smiles from the inside out for a brighter future.

29. My Christmas Blessings

I have always believed in the magic of Christmas and the special warmth in people's hearts. The last Christmas was more profound for me than usual. My daughters had arranged to have a three-foot Christmas stocking dropped off at my room in the Marian villa nursing home. It was totally unexpected, and my feelings of profound gratitude played out with a surge of lip-trembling, humbling tears. Not because of the gifts, but because they took the time to figure out a way to make me feel even more loved and special than I already did. It is what you do for others that expands the love in your heart; that is why it is more blessed to give than to receive.

Also, this Christmas, I learned how much my grandchildren care about me, and how it tugs at their little hearts that I am not able to walk yet.

Jared, my 4-year-old grandson said to me, "Grandma, I would give up anything if you could walk again." He paused as if trying to find something worthy of trading, and then he added, "Even my house."

Among all the toys and surprises of Christmas, here was this dear, sweet boy, trying to find a way to help me. My heart warmed as I received this unexpected gift of familial love. This reminded me of the little drummer boy, giving the gift of music to baby Jesus because that was all he had to give.

My third blessing on that wonderful day was my great-grandson Tyson. His grandma needed something to sit him in because she did not have his chair with her, so she improvised with the use of an oval laundry basket that was padded with pillows. Candy plunked our four-month-old bundle of joy down. Smiling angelically, he molded comfortably into his new location. It was like seeing baby Jesus in the manger in front of the Christmas tree, offering to the world his beautiful smile of innocence. God does work in mysterious ways.

30. Lessons in Life

Since I've been in this chair, it has been like a period of enlightenment. My legs are not yet working properly, so I'm forced to stay immobile except for where I can travel with my wheelchair. I must now count on others to help me get washed and dressed, to shop for me, to accompany me on outings and to attend to any other concerns I may have.

I have learned the gift of patience. Anyone who is disabled knows how long the wait can be for a pair of helping hands. Grumbling and criticism are toxic. I have learned how to replace them with an attitude of gratitude, gifting others with respect and appreciation for their skills.

When the time is long, I meditate and redirect my focus to my surroundings, taking notice of the colours, sights and sounds in close proximity to me. I must appreciate each moment and learn from it. I must ask myself questions to find out how the situation fits in my walk of life. By doing this, my personal filing system is strengthened, my awareness heightened.

When staff members are in a foul mood, it is hard not to take it personally. I must force myself to remember that there is a lesson or message in everything—be it good or not so favorable. It makes me aware of my shortcomings, if I choose to take heed. I am a bit judgmental at times, and I voice my opinion when I should keep my thoughts inside my head. That way, there are no regrets. The universe is forcing me to assess myself, to learn, to grow.

31. Moving to Cheshire

It was a different world for me. It was the first time in 23 months that I was living on my own again, in my own apartment. I felt liberated. I could conduct myself however I pleased, as long as I was available for the scheduled visits from the Cheshire staff and followed the rules. I started to cook for myself again. No more hospital food for me! The staff would come in and peel potatoes or slice veggies or shred cheese or do anything that I needed as long as it was in their policy to do so. It was a wonderful time for me. I started to think of myself as differently able, not disabled. I got excited about having a sewing room again and having my grandchildren stay overnight. I could even have someone come over for a beer if I wanted.

I was thinking about the creative sewing that I did before I fell, recycling outdated styles into something useful. I think my most prized project was a denim slipcover that I made for my couch. I was given a sofa bed that was in good condition, but the fabric that covered it was quite ugly. It was not in my budget to have it recovered, so I decided to recover it using denim jeans that I had accumulated. I had the knowledge from working in an upholstery shop for four years as a sewer. I was on a creative high as I formulated my plan. I cut the legs off of 16 pairs of jeans, just below the seat of the pants, split them open and started sewing one to another, forming a pattern of light and dark as I sewed. I was careful to fit the pieces together snugly as I crafted my creation. I made the cover all one piece so it would not need to be straightened each time someone sat on it. I made separate covers for the cushions: one side was light denim, and the other side was dark denim, so I could vary the appearance from time to time. I was so proud of my accomplishment. I knew that there was not another like it in the whole world. I wish that I had sent the story to a women's magazine for publication, but I didn't.

Now that I am in this wheelchair, I lack movement, not creativity.

I got along with the staff, and I enjoyed their visits, except for one lady with whom I rubbed edges. I found that, when she was doing my care, it was better if I didn't speak. After all, when I did speak up, she would ask, "Why did you say that?" When I didn't speak, she would say, "Why aren't you speaking to me?" It was so frustrating. I wasn't trying to be insulting or antisocial. When it was shower day, I asked her to close the bathroom door because I got cold easily.

She would say, "I can't stand it; I'm too hot."

She was there to do my care, so I talked to her supervisor about her and asked whether I could have a different caregiver. I was told that they used to do that, but they didn't anymore. In short, I was told that I would have to work it out on my own.

I was a little shaken by this response, but I weighed the pros and cons of being there and decided to do my best.

After two years of waiting, my insurance claim for my fall finally came through. But when the Cheshire coordinator found out, it turned my world upside down again. She said she was going to charge me $6,000 per month for my care and rent.

I said, "I don't think so!" But I was in a bind and didn't know what I was going to do. Later, I went to Parkwood for therapy and met up with a lady named Daphne. She told me that she had her own house and would rent me a room and provide a caregiver for only $1,800 per month. (She was a paraplegic as well, so she needed her own caregivers.) She also said that I would have my very own attendant. This all sounded pretty good to me, and given my options, it seemed like the best course of action.

I moved in the following month and regretted every day that I was there. She was a shyster. It was like jumping from the pot into the fire. Not only did I not have my own attendant, the time allotted was shared with two other clients. This meant that I did not get the care I was promised. I was lucky if I got a minimum amount of care. As a result, I suffered from reoccurring bladder infections again, which drained all my strength and played havoc with my body because of an endless string of antibiotics that I had to consume.

This was not right, and it was very unhealthy for me, so I asked my daughters to look for a place for me. Within two months, I was able to move into my own house and put that bad experience behind me.

32. 62 Edmunds Crescent

On November 22, 2009, for the first time, I was able to go inside the house that I had bought. Before that, I wasn't able to get in because I am in a wheelchair and needed a ramp. I rolled inside the kitchen and was in awe. I ruled the roost! I was the head honcho and sole proprietor of this little piece of heaven.

There were a lot of renovations to be done to make it wheelchair accessible for me. Luckily, my daughter's boyfriend, Derek, was a handyman. He tore down walls, remodeled cupboards and replaced flooring until everything was adjusted to my needs. On December 5, 2009, I moved into my very own house.

It was a little scary for me at first. It was great that I was getting a somewhat normal life, but I was also responsible for hiring my own staff to perform my care. I put an ad on Kijiji for attendant care. I prayed every day that the universe would send me good-quality people to be my new employees.

I would like to say that it all went great, but that would be a total fib. Most of the applicants were sincere, but there were a few that really tested my faith and resourcefulness.

There was one girl—I will call her Sue—who seemed to be a perfect match at first. She was warm and friendly, and she seemed competent at her job. I gave her my speech about always showing up on time, about calling me ahead of time if she couldn't make it. I also explained how important it was that she finished the shift and not leave before it was over. I noted that, if she had to leave, I would expect her to find a replacement. I had all my new employees sign a contract of awareness, as I called it. It states the rate of pay, the issue of insurance and the fact that I am in a vulnerable state.

She was scheduled to work the very first night in my home. The night went smoothly, but when it was time to get me up in the morning, she said, "I don't feel well, and I don't feel good enough to transfer you. Can you get someone else?"

I was horrified! I asked her to bring me the phone so I could try to find a replacement, which she did. My first three calls were met with rejection, and my list was short. While I was trying to find someone, I hollered between calls, "Are you okay?"

There was no answer. She had left without saying a word. She left me, a quadriplegic in my bed, home alone.

Finally, I found someone who could come in to finish the shift. Fortunately, I had my door opener in my purse, so I could let her in.

I had Sue's number in my purse so I called her home number. I wasn't expecting her to answer. When she picked up, I said, "What happened? You left without saying a word!"

She said, "I'm calling the doctor as we speak." I didn't believe her.

That was the beginning of three months of hell. During that time, I spent five nights in my chair because workers did not show up or call to say that they were not coming (or it was a long weekend and I could not get anybody on such short notice). It was by the grace of God that I got through all that.

Things seemed to be going well until I discovered that someone was stealing from me. I opted to terminate her employment immediately. She was only taking small amounts at a time at first so I wouldn't notice, but over the span of a few months, it added up to $1,200—that I knew about.

I liked this girl and thought I could trust her, but I was wrong. When I sat Sharon down to give her the final pay. I told her that she was fired because she stole from me. She turned on her fake tears and said that she would never do something like that. She told me that she loved working for me! And in the very next breath with the use of some extremely expletive adjectives she demanded that I pay her now!" She added to that: "You are putting me and my children out on the street. I made it clear to her that I was not the one who stole.

Spring is now in the air, though, and I can get outside and enjoy my beautiful yard. I have a pond filled with fish that sets the mood for serenity, and I also have a six-foot-tall ceramic angel that watches over my place. She stands in the middle of my flowerbed offering peace and love to everyone. I can sit out here and see all the good this place has to offer.

33. The Surgery of Hope

In May of 2011, I underwent another surgery. They took a piece of my intestine and made it into a tube that went from the bladder to the belly button. This is referred to as a cassel valve stoma. The purpose of this surgery was to make it more comfortable for me and allow me to self-catheterize. No longer would I void through the urethra, the urine would now come up the cassel valve stoma and out through the belly button. A draining hose called a catheter was inserted down the tube until the urine flowed. This procedure was designed by Dr. Patrick Luke, at University Hospital in London, Ontario.

I thought the concept was good, and I saw the humour in it: I could now pee like a boy—and I couldn't wait to write my name in the snow. Sadly, that little caper didn't work.

My body was in shock for a year and a half, and I struggled with infections that drained me to the core. I had little energy, and all I wanted to do was sleep. I would make some progress in therapy, standing and stepping, and then, without warning, another bout of infections would hit, causing me to faint and babble like a possessed demon.

One morning, when my worker, Sarah, was putting me in the shower, I fainted. I woke up at the hospital in the emergency department. I had contracted Pseudomonas, which is a bacteria that affects compromised tissue in the body. These are infections resulting from treatment in the hospital. It took ten days in the hospital, hooked up to an aggressive IV medication, to get it under control. And then, approximately six months later, it happened again, but I only had to be hospitalized for four days.

Since the surgery, it is much easier for me to catheterize on my own. My hands are still curled and tight—and I do struggle at times—but I can do it.

34. Messages in Rocks

It is November of 2010, I am sitting here in my living room, by the east window, enjoying the warmth of the sun and looking at my beautiful, polished rocks that Candy gave me.

They all have words written on them. The words are: *Faith, Hope Believe, Gratitude, Abundance,* Grandma, *Faith* (again) and *Luck.* They are arranged in this order to convey a message. When we want anything in our lives, we must start out with *faith* (knowing that we can and will receive what we ask for). Next is *hope* (we hope that our desires will manifest the way we envision them, and when and if they do, they are right for us). The biggest rock that I have is- *Believe* (you need belief to fuel all the others, and to feed the quest of life). The next is *Gratitude* (this one is light pink and shiny, and it triggers thoughts of well-being, like the beauty of a delicate flower). Next to it is *Abundance* (it is flat, polished and oval and when you have all the previous attributes, abundance is certain—to me, abundance is a perception of your life as it is; the gift of a positive attitude is mine). Beside *abundance* is a heart-shaped, polished gem with the word *Grandma* on it (it is a wonderful blessing of timeless love). At this point, there is *faith* again (this one is white and easier to read—as you go through life and manifest many blessings, it is easier for faith to grow). The final rock is Luck (when you have faith, hope and belief in progress, and it comes to pass, we call it *luck*).

I want to be like a rock, strong enough so life doesn't wear me down too fast, mysterious enough so everything about me is not obvious, but adaptable enough that I would fit in anywhere.

35. Leaves of Positive Change

I have a three-foot-square, abstract, wire leaf collection on my wall that immediately captures one's attention. The leaves are metallic, green, brown and gold. The light from the window illuminates them like an electric light show. I immediately gave it meaning and purpose in my collection and made up the following poem about it:

Leaves of Positive Change

Leave negative behaviour in the past.
Leave thoughts of inadequacy out of your daily programming.
Leave criticism and gossip out of your communications.
Leave smiles and blessings of positive energy for everyone you meet.
And leave them with words of hope and encouragement.

PART V

Worth Sharing

What follows is a collection of poems, words of encouragement, helpful expressions and anything else that I wanted to share.

I wrote the following poem a few years ago when I was going through hard times. Heartache piles up, especially when I think of my son, Jade, who died the day he was born. I did not even get to hold him. My daughter Carrie died tragically at age 2. I never got to see her grow up. My dear, troubled granddaughter Alysia took her own life at age 13, she had to deal with some horrific circumstances; she felt too much pain in her life and did not realize her worth.

I had no idea that I was healing myself. It's a healing called head-heart-hand therapy. It is a technique used when a person is grieving. You write about what is bothering you to transfer the pain in your heart and the thoughts in your head to words on the page to ease the pain.

Yesterday's Kiss

This pain is not me;
It is a mere illusion of my fears.
This sadness is not me;
It is only my soul clearing itself with tears.
The heaviness that surrounds me
Is just energy from another place.
It lands upon the frowns on my face.
The circumstance of bliss

Is gone like yesterday, like a stolen kiss.

I allow these feelings to surface,

But they cannot stay.

I put everything into perspective when I pray.

I got the idea for the following poem one night while partying with my sister-in-law and friend, Renée. The first verse just fell on the paper easily with each sip of beer. I just kept asking myself, *what else does the elbow do?* As a song, I would want Toby Keith to sing it to the tune of "Red Solo Cup," a very popular country song.

THE ELBOW BENDING BLUES

I got the elbow-bending blues
I just keep drinking all this booze
My belly keeps getting bigger
I'm going to lose my figure,
I got the elbow bending blues!

I went to the mall
I didn't need much at all
My elbow started bending
I was doing a lot of spending
I was buying everything I could grab,
My car was full and had to call a cab!
But, I only needed shoes.
I got the elbow bending blues!

I stopped at an Italian restaurant to try their pasta
My elbow started bending,
I had to eat faster
I cleaned up my plate!

And ordered double salad and cake,
My arm was getting tired, and my face began to ache
I got the elbow-bending blues!

My garden needed attention
There were too many weeds to mention
My elbow started bending fast,
The weeds were going to last!
My arms began to ache
Oh! For pity's sake!
I pulled out all the flowers!
And it only took an hour
I got the elbow-bending blues!

I went to the gym
To work on getting slim
I was in a rut!
I needed to trim my butt,
My feet were moving and my elbows were bending,
I work so hard my pants needed mending.
I got the elbow-bending blues

I have maxed out my credit card
My house is full of wares and no room in my yard
I have too much to eat!
I can't see my feet!
But I think I finally beat
The elbow-bending blues!

I received this letter from Renée on February 17, 2011. I had sent her a gift after the tragic death of her only son, and this is the thank-you note I received back:

Dear Linda,

Thank you for the love, friendship and generosity. There are no words I can use that will express how this made me feel. It is with great pride that I call you my sister. I hope you know how much you mean to me.

You never cease to amaze me. This past year has been rough for me, and this journey of pain is not over. I tried to take it one day at a time, but sometimes several days attack me all at once, and then I'm down for the count for a while. The only thing that eases my pain is -knowing that you are there for me. Where I lack strength, is where you shine. I am doing the best I can, but I also know I can't do it alone.

There is no doubt in my mind that I have the best support family anyone could ever ask for, and for that, I thank you. You are one of my earth angels.

My love always,
Renée

This letter really touched me. Even in a time of grieving, she took the time to express her thanks. We all need each other for support and appreciation in life.

I wrote this poem in 2010. I wanted to express
to my family what their support means to me.

Christmas

Christmas is a time for sharing,
I'm so blessed with a family that is caring.

Each child of mine is a gift of love,
Packaged as an earth angel from above.

I have all the gifts I need from the ones I hold so dear—
Hugs to comfort me and calm my fear.

Laughter to energize and brighten my being,
Love and assistance for the needs that I am seeing.

Let's not forget the grandchildren, who fill the days with
innocence and wonder and touch my heart
with the love of Jesus from the start.

These are the gifts that are blessings from above,
Every day is Christmas when you have family love.

My gift to my family is an attitude of gratitude for all you do.
My heart flutters with emotion, and I know that it's true.

I am determined to walk again, and I know that it is no easy feat. I have become my own cheering squad. I wrote the following poem to help me stay focused:

When I Am Better

I won't give up on my dreams to walk again.
Fate is stacked against me, it seems.
The doctor's words of gloom, I block from my mind—
I inject affirmations of the healing kind.
I feel myself happy and in control;
I won't let setbacks take a toll.
I will walk, and I will drive.
I believe, therefore I am.
In God's time, not mine,
I reap the benefits of the divine—now and when I am better.

Words That I Find Motivating

I find affirmations helpful to keep my mind focused on what I'm trying to accomplish. Beyond a shadow of a doubt, this is my favorite, most inspiring and encouraging one:

"Whatever I vividly imagine, ardently desire, sincerely believe and enthusiastically act upon, must inevitably come to pass."

(Just to personalize this affirmation, I add *chooka! chooka!* at the end for effect.)

I created this little play on words:

I am not able to tie a knot (not) at this time, so I am not disabled. (This helps me avoid taking myself too seriously.)

"Keep your chin up!" is a powerful statement. As I mentioned before in this book, my dad said these words on a few occasions. It forced me to look up from the tightening hurt of heartache, and when I did, I saw all those around me who loved and cared about me, and it reminded me of a higher power that governs all our lives. This leads me to another statement: "Change your seeing, and you will change your scene."

"It's okay to be down sometimes—even the sun goes down every day, but it always comes back up."

This quote explains to me why I love bright, yellow happy-face stickers: they remind me of the sun coming up and allow me to look forward to a new day of wonder.

I've also started having the following exchange with anyone who will play along:

"Guess what?"

"What?"

"Something wonderful is going to happen today!"

This puts you in a happy place to start your day, and something good always happens, whether you realize it or not. Once you train yourself to think this way, it becomes as addictive as Tim Horton's coffee.

My next expression of optimism will be a bumper sticker that says the following: "Life is good, and happy rocks!"

By the time this book reaches the stores, I will be promoting my dvd about my life. I am in the process of setting up a web page as well. I invite everyone who reads my book to send me a message telling me how these pages may have brightened your day, and helped to keep you positive and counting your blessings every day.

(Please put- Keep Your Chin Up in the subject line)

Thank you!

lindalendt@gmail.com

Printed in the United States
By Bookmasters